G000147642

MAPPING THE LIGHT

OTHER PUBLICATIONS BY AUTHOR:

Vortices
An Unfinished Sufficiency
Another Morning of Quiet Pleasures
The Silence Unheard
Goater's Alley
A Lope of Time
Where Acid Has Etched

Echoes From The Steppe

Without Skin: Interviews with 23 Internationally Renowned
Women Poets

MAPPING THE LIGHT

RUTH O'CALLAGHAN

Shoestring  Press

All rights reserved. No part of this work covered by the copyright herein may be reproduced or used in any means – graphic, electronic, or mechanical, including copying, recording, taping, or information storage and retrieval systems – without written permission of the publisher.

Printed by imprintdigital
Upton Pyne, Exeter
www.digital.imprint.co.uk

Typesetting and cover design by narrator
www.narrator.me.uk
info@narrator.me.uk
033 022 300 39

Published by Shoestring Press
19 Devonshire Avenue, Beeston, Nottingham, NG9 1BS
(0115) 925 1827
www.shoestringpress.co.uk

First published 2018
© Copyright: Ruth O'Callaghan
© Cover image: Christine Johnson

The moral right of the author has been asserted.

ISBN 978-1-912524-04-4

For Christine

Without those love and encouragement
this book would never have happened

CONTENTS

Noting Inconsistencies

CAMERA

How shall we frame this city?
Wide-lensed to incorporate the Abbey and Paul's.
No! Swing to vertical for the corporate Shard.
Crick a neck? I'd rather cock a snook.
Like the orators in disused doorways?
You mean the disregarded?
Then regard the indigenous white.
Or Paddy…. Or Mohammed. Finger-frame them!
Finger Paddy? Frame Mohammed?
Surely not with judgment, rule of law?
Order! Order!
Is that the ordure of a politician?

1.

We hear laughter—rain-drains gurgling underground or is it…
THEM?   We hear but
    fear they may flood these very streets,
    street after concrete street, no soak-away.
    Houses are mere stubble in a landscape where city
    skyscrapers sway as wheat in wind.
Why do we stay? Why do we wait

    in an agitation of dark,
    waiting for an assertion
    of… light?
    a slink…?

2.

As yet the holy host
of sun has not risen
on the contiguity of bodies, hooded faces hidden
disgorged

from doorways opening inward.
Here, at the last stop on the line
waiting for the return tram

sorrow sharp as sorrel
infuses. Here the unworded
may question

this stump of time lent to us: is it to be finger-flicked
gutterward, a spent butt a beggar
may retrieve

or consumed frugally whilst noting inconsistencies
as in the language of strangers.

Although we speak of transparencies we camouflage
desire in a deluge
of reprisal, regret

not that which was not
offered but that which was.

3.

After, there was the slow unveiling
of each callous act: the cage
ejecting the bird...

4.

…into a wordless country where winter's
crisp knitting leaves uncertain the placing
of foot or thought. An unattended moment,
eyes sliding toward the distant distraction
of the rook's parched cry on a clip of wind
serves to advance the slip toward unsafe
ground, toward the unguarded word: truth
twice-distilled in fly-posted doorways, free
to all, to those who huddle, to those who
hurry past with averted eyes, recalcitrant,
ignoring the seven degrees of separation.

5.

He would. He would walk. Fast. Walk fast though
perfidious light loops his legs, entangles, though
breath bursts in his chest, blocks mouth, though
mouth now—stopped? Eyes? Stopped? Though
Blinden. Bl... Blind! Burning he will walk though

trees shed fires before his feet, though
flames leap, blister, blacken, though
his feet blacken, black as... though
he will not think of...black, though
thought black, congealed, though

blood black, congealed, though
runnels of blood, gut... though
he needs skin to... t... though
skin is too thin, if it... though
if it cannot contain... though

blood is dammed... though
thought is not.... Though
blood-thought.... Though
that will damn. Though
damned, even though
damned, he will walk.

6.

You will not wait so dark cloaks you, marks you
with a lash of rain, your silk mac
streaks black

clings to your chest while traffic slows before you
stills the way a word may be held
in the head

the way comfort in the inarticulate soothes you
the tyre's susurrus rhythmic as the sound
of sea

or the slow release
of bubble within the lava lamp
the wax warmed, rising through the cool of your
clear glass, light increasing heat. Incandescent. Cyclical.

LOVE SECTIONS

When the magi came for her she did not move
the baby slung loosely over a shoulder unwilling
to release him to the confines of the pen.
Her blanched fingers swab the door frame,
dribble bleach from a drum standing sofa high:
        Not to be taken internally:
        Keep well away from children.

When the dark doctor smelling of olibanum coughs,
the mother sashays backward, shoots
a killing stream of germicide from her child bearing hip.

The social worker finger-tickles the baby's splayed foot
unaware his cold wedding ring curves
the pliant body. Lovingly the mother scours the spot.

The psychiatrist helps stash once worn baby clothes
into sacks as big and black as body bags. Well-worn
words ease the baby from her arms, persuade her
the germs are snared, straitening the mother's love:
        Not to be taken internally
        Keep well away from children.

ENLIGHTENMENT

Settled in shadow she wraps worn grass
around ribs that arc.

She knows the healing balm of nettles
that soothe each wound.

She knows, too, the secrets of spiders
who inherit webs

but it was the robin who wrested that particular
one from her

who broadcast it as if the ordinary is more.
A professor told her

now *they* employ wasps to sting the air
to bring news of the silent snow.

Indigenous

The light deepens, riffles the blind
windows of close-shut houses huddled
in garden-less streets

where a cat's shadow
plays over reclaimed brick, a makeshift
kennel emits *yip yip* betraying

the puny, waking the woman who dares
beyond these whitened walls, the thin
thread of her curse fluting the air.

ARLENE

Will you get your lardy arse out of my bed
to be seen at the labour? There's jobs to be had
and bread to be put on the table. Oh, you were able
last night with the malt and the fine words to weasel your way
into my bed, much good that did me. You're all mouth and trousers
but when the old whisky hits it's that flab dick shows the true man.
Give Flyboy his due, God rest him, he knew how to treat a lady,
could sink his drink with the best of 'em and still do his duty,
the black stuff glistening his 'tache in the rise and fall of it…
You'll never be half the man… are you listening?

DEREK

He was a man who had never curled
the four corners of a handkerchief over
his bald spot on a beach where a tide

retreated, leaving only a distant stretch
of mudflats shining in his monocular vision.
She had only an eye for him. The bald spot

on her fur coat hid a bold heart. Loving the curl
of his toes that dug deep into the dark squelch,
the way he let lug worms slide over his skin,

she shed her fur, bundled skirt into the fine lace,
she was a best knickers every day kind of girl,
and lay back—knowing old wood burns slow.

DONNA

It was hot. It was seven a.m. The siren already demanding.
I was fourteen. Confessed to sixteen when they demanded.
The lie held. They needed my hands. I needed their money.
Collusion in the flicker of an eye to flip-flop tops, pork pies,
meat pies, apple pies, the illusion of variety happily sought
in the so-grey suet that slithered in the dust, the gravy spilt.
Flanking the conveyor belt we moaned to *Workers Playtime*,
examined the varicose veins of Florrie, forty years standing,
covered at clock-in, when the super snooped, for Vi juggling
husband home from a war that let him share his nightmares
with neighbours five houses away and served to remind her
father of the war before: gas, the stench of his trench foot,
amputated, uncompensated by hand-propelled wheelchair,
adapted, left hand drive, his right lost to a friendly grenade,
and then her mother—broken as the doll she always carried:
little wonder it was always Vi first to touch Joan's hunchback
for luck, to wring Vera's three fingers, place spit on Wall-Eye
servicing the belt, despite having to swerve his early morning
hard-on—he'd shed it behind a delivery van to the yardmen's
whistles and Elsie's *Dirty Bugger*. Thirty-three buck-toothed
years on the job with a daily axe to wield, I avoided her eye.
I knew she knew I was in Milly's class, her daft daughter's kid.
I'm backward, I claimed. *Daft on the right side*, she snorted,
willing to bide her time for the favour she'd be bound to ask.

LAZARUS

Light, right angled, scratches at a bowed window
silty from jack-hammer grit, leaving lace shadows
on a newspaper cloth splotted already with black
market bacon fat. A scald of words passes over

his ears the way each season passed its light
over the schoolroom, a length of days unspool,
definite with expectation, denying confined time,
denying ma's (and his) rosary-fingered nights.

She mapped heaven knowing stars shine brightest
when it's darkest and this she had written, crabbed
hand mottling the page, to his unknown destination,
repeated again, again, again, in a voice lambent

as her rubescent face at his first communion, spoke
of spring when the half of him was deposited swiftly
on her step: evaded seepage from his loose bag.
He cannot tell her the feel of light warns of winter.

HOME GUARD

Here comes the other army, the elderly beige
dragging cloth shopping bags past a gape
where houses stood, twisted as the stoop
of old women intent on day-hardened bread.

In this rinse of day a wind-shrink body mutters
his Co-op divi number over and over, shakes
his stick at the advancing Bosch, droops by
a bench abused by lovers the night before,
the coil of dark lending a sheen to the dull
de-mob suit but that was a different war, he
snatches at childhood *Frog went a-courting,*
forgets the fact the cat ate the couple, grips
his coupons (rationing such as Kitchener
never knew pointing a finger directly at you)
shouts his army number 1093…3? 3…?…
or is it the divi and is that gas in the wind?

Mother Copage, curlers accordion-pleated,
scoops the last bag of broken from under
Siobhan O'Flaherty's outstretched hand,
a dried-mud smile cracks her face, scorns,
May your daughter never marry a navvie.

THE SUNSET HOME FOR THE ELDERLY
PURCHASES MORE CHAIRS

Side by side they parade, one upright, square backed
but for a slight slope around the shoulders, a measure
against which the droop of age furling forward toward
the facing regiment who nod-rock to snores, quavers,
minds still stepping down Brockley way—Rivoli style!

Migrations

SIOBHAN

Will you lean into this morning, she said.
Wash yourself, watch yourself, there's those
who wish you harm though, God love them,
their mothers didn't teach them the right
from the wrong if ever they knew themselves,
but they're swift with the flick and the comb
is sharpened steel so don't you be thinking
he'll be dressing the grease of that hair.
If he catches your eye don't stare, walk by
with your eye dropped. Don't strut. Or wave
your spade or do that finger thing. Never mind
about Shakespeare and his archers of Agincourt
he isn't our Yeats. Was he there at the Boyne?
Were they Catholic? The famine still holds so
don't be bringing home that Bardolph or Nym
they'll be leading you astray. Or the other feller,
who in God's name would call their child Pistol?
And don't be giving the gaffer any ould chat
or he'll be sending you back on the next boat.
Not like your poor uncle Flynn. Will you listen!

And here he is, hod flung careless across
a scrawn of shoulder, his toothless whistle

He came to be a soldier, a soldier, a soldier
He came to be a soldier in McAlpine's Fusiliers.

Broken-backed, broken hearted but never broken,
the hopes high while the drink flows, when his drink's low
stand him a glass, Finbarr Flynn O'Brien has served his time,
the brick dust of his days ground into a haze, shaking
from *The Nowhere Inn* to *The Leper's Lights*, clinging
foot after treacherous foot to the paving that wavers
toward the spike, Arlington House or the Rowton,
he'll lay his head wherever he can, Camden, Fulham,
his hod now empty but the head full of him barefoot,
bare-arsed, steadying his load heavy with dreams,

 I'll take ye home again, Kathleen

with the fortune made and a farm to be had but for now
heft the hod, skip the miss of rung that did for Flyboy,
don't eye the gaffer's piece or the fist on the head
Chancer Lavelle had to his cost will be yours
with marching orders but Finbarr's marching days
are done, all he seeks is a corner to peel back a boot,
stretch a suppurating leg that trips Victor slicking back
dandruff onto the velvet of his Drape. His elephant's quiff
quivers as he bends, whispers *You're a fuckin' filthy fucker.*
Finbarr smiles. Appreciates a tongue teaser, a teasing tongue,
a tongue twister, a twist of tongue, of knife in a summer street,
the glint hidden in the ribcage but mirrored in the steel of comb
as Victor bends, retrieves his flick, meticulously avoids blood
on his blue suedes to step over an old man mustering his past
Ödegard was right, Lavelle, emanatin' needs a 'g'. Fine words
we shared back then. Kiss me, Cassidy, Kathleen's dead.
I'll show I know liminality of life. And there they find him…
  Dom… Dom… Dom.

26

CONGRESS

Lavelle knew it was crucial
Ödegard thought it essential
Cassidy, crestfallen, liminal,

the argument unkempt
enough to unseal bony bodies
cross-hatched with scars,

rumps clay-red, crumpling
pants wet-darkened,
fingers podging the air

to a pulse
of expletives/deletions,
the caul of thought

a craft frail as skelf;
tropes, palimpsestic,
ravelled with scarcity

lethal in intent,
flinched from each tongue
as first one then a third

declared the day
transubstantiated, its digestion
eating the wolf in all of us

leaving the one question
—the fulfilling of it—
crucial, essential, liminal.

COURTIN'

It is so! Lavelle cried, rubbing a rag over two-tone shoes
recently blagged from an American in search of ancestors,
his lash of joy still bletting the air at having his Irish heritage
now assured by Chancer Lavelle claiming second cousin,
twice removed, on the mother's (God rest her soul) side.
It is so! Lavelle repeated. *Mary Finegan will be at the bus,
her night shift finished and I'll drift by, oh, so slow, in these.
She'll note, in that way that nurses have, the shine on them
and I'll court her with their being dull compared to the light
in her fine…. No! I'll say, emanatin' from her fine eyes.
A wondrous word, emanatin'. A word to roll around a tongue.
A tongue should foster such a word, such a word being fit
for a king. This word will make me king of Mary Finegan
being a word to spawn love in the heart, indeed any part,
of any woman alive or dead so's youse both be scarce away.
Take this day I'm givin' you, I'm givin' you it freely but if you
have a bob or two in case we need a jar before we begin….*
Emanatin'? said Cassidy, crestfallen. *Good man. Emanatin'.*
It needs a 'g', said Ödegard. A 'g' is an essential component
to the proceedings. An educated man, a man fit to court a nurse,
will have a 'g' about him. Being without a 'g' is like being a king
without a 'dom'. Without one you may be a king but ye'll be still
be in need of a 'dom'. No woman will want a man, king or not,
without his 'dom'. *Don't you be begetting lecturing me, I need
no lecturing on begetting,* cried Lavelle, patting his top pocket.

WRITING BACK

His letters slanted toward to the left,
shrank away from the edge of page
where a new line had to be confronted,

the cheap sheet absorbing the ink
blurs the creep of words reluctant
to accost that place where their years,

interlocked, would now be picked apart.
The start-stop of courtship: cycling back
from wayside dances, the crossbar-flow

of taffeta catching the tread of his tyres,
a midnight kitchen heavy with the promise
of tomorrow's bread—yeast trapped, rising—

where his one kiss, stolen, brought her
close but the web of her smile threatened
fleeing him out of the door into sour light

over the monotonous mountains. A scree
of thoughts cancels his smile as he licks
the envelope alive with spiders of Quink.

DOUBLE CUT

He's there again at the roadside, never lifting
his head to hoots or waves, wheelchair wedged
by stones that block the roll forward but not
the view back to where the road straggles

the peat bog, to the days where the *sleán*'s
haft caressed the palm of his father waist-deep
in a pit, feet braced to carve and curve each
brick of black gold to the waiting barrowman.

While his child-thread of muscle through hand
to foot hardened, he'd lift the peat iron to practise
his swing, a winged blade slicing the bedroom air,
tales of the fourteen hour day with twenty boxes

cut and turned to the wind for the drying, turned
impatient a boy to be a man, to heft each one to *his*
barrowman, and yes, when the time came he knew
he'd cut twenty-two, leaving *his* son to balance

home the rusted bike, a creel of sods for the firelight
to flicker faces as night drew day nearer.
                                          The feel
of the *sleán* still in his hand he claws at the wheel,
curses sharp stones guarding him from the road.

UN-   UNDER

skilled   rated

a hoddie for two brickies, three if need be,
wets mortar boards on the scaffie, agrees
aggregates with cement till one colour only,
centres the mix, adds water, turns constantly,
then readies his hod, his box of three sides,
delivers stacks from pallet, twelve bricks a go.

loved   valued

Joe Loss, Dead Loss, kept strict three-four time until
the foxtrot's risqué glide when *she* led Finbarr outside,
fingers insistent stripped him senseless, she wordless,
him witless but clumsy with urgency he tried to please,
defeated by suspenders he lost his load, her screech
knelling his name, her derision denied the trying again.

housed   mined

No word wasted. Her finger points towards the illiterate
hand. Finbarr, noting another NO on the flyblown paper,
ponders deeply how the Irish still maintain their position
below dogs and now blacks.

When the rest of the world arrives
will we remain shut out, your house rebuilt by dint of my
three-sided hod? Will I find rest only in my four sided box

UNDERGROUND?

FINBARR FLYNN READS BECKETT'S
WHOROSCOPE

Jay-sus! This man's all academics and eggs.
Sophistry in a riff of Aristotle, Descartes, Galileo,
a passing glance at Hal —with the slightest pry
into sly Augustine's revelation in a shrubbery,
was he peripatetic and priapic?—before aiming
a well-shod boot at the brothers Boot to boot.
He reports *the shuttle of a ripening egg combs
the warp of his days* but is this a necessary
precursor to refutation of a doctrinal Jansenist
or is timing in the anal ejection of the egg reliant
upon Galilean movement removing responsibility
from God's own creature specifically constructed
for the purpose to shite a sought-after food source
or will he accept the Copernican theory, some say
gobshite, the kiss of transubstantiation on his lips?

VALEDICTION

i.m. Finbarr Flynn O'Brien

He was an educated man. He read Beckett.
Could *critique*, his word, Beckett's horoscope.
Beckett? But did he appreciate the Bard?
Beckett? He'd quote you, chapter and verse.
Of the Bard? To be or not…. Hamlet?
Beckett smoked Havanitos Planteros.
But you said he was an educated man.
Does that disqualify you? I'd best be careful.
You said he was an educated man….
Not Beckett. Finbarr Flynn O'Brien. A sensitive man.
…one who would mourn Ophelia, know Cordelia was…?
The knowing of her was mutual. He'd never thrust…
so's to speak, himself where he was not wanted.

RED FOX PRESS—ACHILL
(Found After Finbarr's Death)

for Francis from Finbarr

In this book of Beckett's poems there is a note
referring to l.3 on p.3
the poems begin on p. 20 all previous denoted
in the latinate manner
even the editor's note is vii with introduction ix
is this the mayhem
that awaits me when I begin to study his form
and is it the same
as the note you hang outside your gallery door
Come in. We're closed.

As closed as the fist of the foreman who refused his labour.
As closed as the mouth on the woman he so longed to kiss.
As closed as the doors on the streets where he did not live.
As closed as the shop whose doorway lent a night's shelter.
As closed as the ears to the Irish dying in the time of famine.
As closed as the conscience of English absentee landlords.
As closed as the peace between Catholic and Orangeman.
As closed as the eye of a beholder melding money/colour.

QUESTION

What imagined promise
what cause, shaped our dispersion

bearing language
to unfamiliar places? Wind-borne

the seed adapts
to thinner soil but remembers

a rich earth
where roots held deep in the dark

urge return, loosens resolve
to survive in this shallow sediment:

yet displacement demands due toll
refuses reverse-history.

MV MONTE ROSA BEMOANS
TRANSPORTING ELIZABETH

I am from elsewhere. My core is different from yours.
My course has differed from my beginning as yours will.

Yes. Ahm elsewhere but mah core no diffrent yours.
Mah course that diffrent. Ah go travel de open sea,
get me new life. No labour for she morning to night,
she squawking Betsie, Betsie turn down me coverlet,
Betsie, Betsie, brin' me dis, brin' me dat. Brin' now!
Betsie, yo look to the chile he wet, he dirty. Betsie!

I have travelled on open seas, forged a new philosophy
to bring joy and strength to those who labour endlessly.

Mah name Elizabeth after de mudder fo John Baptist.
No de mudder fo her chile. She no like his doo-doo.
Ah gets all de bes' jobs! Ah love him but he stink so!

Die Arbeitskräfte were allocated places in preference
to parasites. Our Leader despises moneyed hook noses.

Ah say, Missie, Ah goin' fo' better life. She say Go!
Ah say, Cow never know use of tail till it drop off.
She say, dey no call yo Rosie Redhead over dere.
Rosie Deadhead. Dat wat dey call you…Ginger!
She no talk. She skin be jus' two shades mo light.
An' we's aaa-lll know where dat come from!

But such a noble gesture was brutally capsized by one
Winston who refused to listen when we sued for peace.

Rosie Redhead? Mah hair. It… bit ginger. Not too much!
But she treat me bad those last days. Den she re'lise
Ah goin'. She lef' wid baby doo-doo. She cry! She sigh!
Ah no hard-hearted Hannah. No sir! Ah try teach her.
But yo no dry a river wiv de torch o' brushwood.

Despite transporting our soldiers safely I was abused,
given as a prize of war and used to carry the enemy.

So here I yam. Gov'ment need me. An' Dwayne.
He dun go learn buses. Yo soljers no back de war.
Dey won den go udder one. Dey protec' Empire.
Dey mudders no happy. Ah's de Empire! An' Dwayne.

Renamed *Windrush* I refuse to accept it but am unable to refuse
passage to those I do not regard. Those who choose migration.

Ah tell Dwayne he black. He big. He goo-ood looking!
Dose white boys look to dere girls. He bes' leave girls.
Man carryin' load o' hay mus' avoid sparks. He lis'en.
He laugh. He say puss an' dogs don' have same luck.
I say, dey see yo wid white girl. Dey 'vite yo? Why?
Cockroach gives party he don' never invite de fowl.

However, I have learnt to conspire with whichever cause.
Acquire secrets. Be party to all their small, futile desires.

They have party in Kingston. No J'macai Kingston.
Kingston, London. a long way fro Brixton. Dey say,
Come, Dwayne. We see yo wid girl. We show you
how show her de lights from de bridge, de light
ova river. He say yo call dis light? Yo no see no light
till yo see mine over de bay. Dey agree. Dey say,
Yeh, boy. Now boy we kick livin' daylights outa yo.

Integration? How mistaken! I was not bothered. I had
delivered my…
load under that assumed name, resumed transportation of soldiers.

De buses was stop nex' day. One minute! Respec'?
One minute? One life? I tol' him! Be discreet.
When yo in donkey yard yo don' mention long ears.
He never lis'en. He do know de ev'ryt'ing. He say,
he never count de fingers wid a four finger man.

Ah say, don' pull dog's tail to see if he be sleep.
But he be youn' man. He test himself. He fail.

1954. My final voyage. My failure. We left Yokohama in high spirits
although laden with stretchers and survivors—the Korean War.

So dis is de better life? De rain it never stop. De house
ain't no house. Half a room, de cooker on de landing
two floors below nex' de toilet. Mah work it never stop.
On'y now it big bums an de doo-doos dey big-big too.
Ah bury mah Dwayne. Mah life. Mah tears never stop.
De landlor' say rent money more. I can' pay. He say Go!
Mischief comes by de pound an goes by de ounce.

Port Said took me eight weeks to achieve, not three. The crew,
                                              such knaves,
grumbled so much I finally exploded! To suffer such ignominy
                                              of being towed
is not in my nature. I am not an ambler! Or craven. When we
                                              made deep water
I sunk my hulk beneath the waves. The gibbering apes of
                                              Gibraltar my witness.

During the 1930s HMT *Empire Windrush* operated as a German cruise
ship under the name *Monte Rosa*. The Nazi regime used her as part of
the *Strength Through Joy* programme to provide cheap holidays as a
means of promoting the party's ideology.

During WW2 she was a German troopship but was taken as a prize
at the end of the war and renamed *Empire Windrush*, transporting
West Indian immigrants to the UK. She continued to be used mainly
as a troopship until March 1954 when she caught fire and sank in the
Mediterranean with the loss of four crew members.

Calibration

THE MORNING AFTER

Vic. Vic! Listen. Last night I had an idea. If we adopt…
Get off! That's all *you* think about. That an' football.
Look. You said we got probs. so if we adopt a dead
old record.… No, not a rock group. A census. 1552.
In Siena. It'll help us work things out.… How? Well,
Mr. Zellinicolini says.… No, I ain't—haven't—been
discussing our probs.…. Or talking. Same thing.
…Don't go there again. We've *been* through all that.
Every bloody—sorry, Mr. Zellinicolini—day. Listen!
There's these Sienese at war with these Florentines,
some old Italian tribes.… *Not* your ACF Fiorentina,
don't think they invented football by then.… Had they?
So Mr. Z was chuntering, he makes it dead interesting,
'n.… O.K. Yeah, they probably would have had a strip
but they call it a coat of arms. Anyway, I thought, 'n I'd
like to discuss… I'm not talking fancy!… it like we do
in class Monday nights.…. I said I hadn't, didn't I?.…
Fancy? Course not. He don't either. It's just I… like,
factory's dead boring 'n that old political bloke, y'know
him who said we've never had it so good when we
were in school 'n I'm still stuck there, in the factory like
when I was a kid 'n bunked off to get some dosh…
I know I still go to school! 'S night school. 'S different.
…I don' know how those old tribes are gonna help me
but it makes you think… 'n question. Mr. Zellinicolini…
I said he didn't, didn't I? So leave it out.… I know you would,
like you did for that poor old sod—sorry again Mr. Z—.
You could've stepped over… If I catch you with that flick!
Don't Donna me! You think you're so big! My hero! *So Not!*
Mr. Zellinicolini says discuss… So what if he's an immigrant?
His English is still better'n yours so I'll *talk* to you then. So.
Siena 'n Florence… They didn't name a city after your mother.
She really wouldn't thank you for thinking she's that old.
Anyway. The census counted mouths 'cos the Florentines…
I don't know if they invented those expensive biscuits…

I know you can go a whole box in one. It counted mouths....
No! Not to see who had eaten the most! For the war effort.
They counted useful mouths, men to fight the Florentines
...You'd do war if they fed you them biscuits? It won't be
some old wino lying around ...'n useless mouths, the old
'n such.... Yeah, that did include women....

                               You know what?
I reckon we got the reverse in this house. All you do is sit
'n guzzle 'n fa... expel wind... *'N you can leave that out!*
What's the use!... Yeah. These are me heels. Yeah. Me reds.
Trainers' for when I'm just sitting with the whole class.
Didn't I say? Mr. Zellinicolini does 1-2-1 drop-ins. Tuesdays....

OBSERVATIONS ON NUMBER 11 BUS

Mullholland! Will ye look at that!
Look at what?
Look at that.
What's that I'm looking at?
That's what I'm telling you.
What's that?
That's what I'm telling you.
Telling me?
To look at that.
Tell-ing me?
What? Yes, I'm tell…

You? Tell-ing me?
To look at that? Out of the window.
TELLING ME?
To look at that! An educated feller would know…
What?
That's why I'm telling ye to look at it… educatedly.
Educatedly?
You are the most educatedly looking feller I know.
I see…. So…. You are requesting that I regard a *rara avis*
that you have failed to decipher but I may do so…educatedly?
What?

You are request…. What is this anomaly, this phenomenon,
this nonpareil, that bemused your uneducated eye?
That feller-me-lad. He's wearing a skirt.
You mean a kilt.
I know a kilt. It's a skirt. And he was holding a man's hand.
Now you're here in England, enlightened England, you must expect
to consider new experiences with a certain degree of sophistication.
Difficult though it may be with your lack of education…
*He was holding a **black** man's hand.*
What? Where? Where? WHERE!
Too late. We've passed them… Mullholland will you please get off my lap….

WARRIOR-SURVIVOR IN OWN LANDSCAPE

Buffered by the doorway
from the wind and whitened night

shrouded in wasteland
between the Colherne and

lights sniping shop mannequins
bunkered in plated glass spraying

the Kings Road
the bones of his rib cage
razored as a bird's beak under

routed traffic choking eastward
honed in the stretch of his

thin tee shirt, faltering

sentinel gaze across
Flanders slime to
                (Passchen....
                (passion

taut under tartan braces
waiting for...

                (The window
                (the window

period to pass.

reflects his scarlet jacket,
beribboned, crowned
by a solitary poppy,

A mandatory moratorium
as he breasts yet another red ribbon:
survival of the unknown

his mind darkens as he rakes
foreign fields for names of those

                (comrades
                (lovers

legion though they were
it was a no names, no pack

(drilled
(drill

into his brain, entrenched
in the weft and memory warp…   entrenched
                                               in the weft and memory
                                               warp…

weaving poppies   *and patchwork*

(in remembrance of the dead beloved.
(in remembrance of the dead beloved.

N.B. The Colherne was a significant pub in the lifestyle of gay men.
During the Aids epidemic patchwork quilts commemorated the lives
of those lost.

The 'window period' is the period of time that it is necessary to wait
before blood can be tested for HIV after having non-safe sex.

S.W.5

An insubstantial day: the rain falling
in its own drear way lending tarmac
sheen once the sun decides to nod
over the Earls Court Road, blinding
beggar and book lover alike—those
seen perusing the very last second
-hand bookshop struggling against
closure, struggling against yet one
more pretzel, pizza, pasta, on-hoof
grease, discarded cardboard he will

discover diving deep into bins while
you dust flour from hands swearing
this liver, to be lightly braised, holds
every ingredient needed to soften,
to whiten them, as you drizzle sun
-flower-and-garlic oil into the crusty-
black pan praying sizzle of visceral
release is not erased but remains
absolute, trapped in his very skin
though he walks, walks in thin rain.

I walk here as much as I can. It's absolutely beautiful even though it's the city. I have a room such as I have always longed for.

Vincent Van Gogh: Stockwell 1873

S.W.9

Blades of paint slashed on walls guided me here.
A warning yes, but a protection also if you believe
the message the crows carved, the curve of beaks
ripping into impasto to reveal the promise the Voice
rejected while Sun, centred among a thrash of crows
circling my head, stilled, gave way to the first throat
of darkness.

> *Don' b'lieve all writin'. Some crazy man*
> *cut off ear like painter 'oo live ova dere long time go.*
> *Yo' hokay? Don' run. No fraid. I your fr'en'. I Aleixo.*

Aleixo! Protector! I knew when he identified himself
I had found my way to my true home, acknowledged
the patience of this very house that had long waited
for the Son of Sons to arrive. I claimed my true name
Arphaxad: Healer. Arphaxad Avishai: Given of God.
The seventh son of the seventh son—ad infinitum—
I am the Way

> *We got squat f yo need bed. Come.*

We entered my house. Even the walls of my house
proclaimed my command: Love you one another.
The crows who had foretold my coming, foretold also
my death with each beak-incision lacerating, each
layer laid bare, revealing that which was prophesied.
Laughter issued as blood from the house: I greeted all
with my Truth

> *You got a right one there, Aleixo. Your call.*

The one who violated my approach crouched at a table
thumbing notes, hands blackened from counting coins,
absorbed in the piles rising beside him, high as Babel.
Before I could smite such desecration he caught my eye
with the can in his hand. Blinded, I allowed Aleixo to lead
me away. I now knew without my Truth they would perish.

> I am their Life

Come, my fr'en'. Come wiv Aleixo.
We fin' you a bed. You safe. I tell you bout my home.
My home, hot. Portagal. We say here is Li'l Portagal.
I mak' you feel my hot sun. It warm you. Then you sleep

The blanket was soiled but I lay down. A loose pipe dripped
water into a bucket, slowly, matching his words, dismantling
my fear as he told of the warmth of his Square, the warmth
of those precious tiles seeped the length of my back, banished
all thoughts of rain as I walked on Pinheiro's stones, drank dark
coffee, consoled Columbano but shunned Assuncão Mangas
when she beckoned…

Here Liz'baff. Liz'baff we haf new fr'en'.

Framed in the doorway a halo of dirt clung to her hair but I knew
that she was not the mother of John. She held out her dark hand.
Do not touch me! She persisted. Reaching toward me. I heard
the crows warning call. Aware the dark one had entered the room
I wrenched the pipe from wall, threw off Aleixo's restraining hand
to strike again and again. Evil covered her face but her soul shone
black as the raven's wing. I fled.

Liz'baff! Liz'baff! Talk a Alexeo!

I will walk. Walk fast. Away from those who pursue,
persecute me. Away from the many who pursue
evil, who trick me with false friendship, pursue
me with their mockery. I will walk fast, pursue
the silver-backed river. I will pursue…. home?

ALEIXO'S SQUARE: AFTER RAIN

The square a seethe of wet and dogs. Awnings, punched,
release all that is gathered there onto the tables swiped
before birdsong each morning by Jose Oliveiro who sniffs
the air, gives thanks to God for what he knows not, notes
rust has reddened the stones laid by Machado PInheiro,
mason, shambles back to the dark that is his constant day.

It is to the air, yes, the air, the God of the Air that Columbano
gives praise, wheezing it into lungs that defy, defeat, no, only
delay the advent of his old friend—who will not come quietly
nor with respect. Columbano is resigned to his final indignity
—hawking onto Pinheiro's intricate design his last lung-blood
as he follows Oliveiro into the constant dark of the café day.

Machado PInheiro masticates. His moustache has long since
fallen short of the flourish of his youth, a time of architectural
aspirations to Manueline proportions and that heavenly body,
Assuncão Mangas, whose ankles now pass at his eye height.
Feckless when younger, she shadows old Columbano, ties up
a dalmatian's spotted length and trips into the day-dark café.

Outside, mistaking it for a tit-bit, the leash strains toward
where Machado Pinheiro pollutes the paving with his phlegm,
for thus are perceptions, whether hound or human, deceived
when desire demands a hunger be assuaged as the mason
could vouchsafe as he too strains towards the so low voices,
seeking from that dark café one that holds his day constant.

Above the café Dorotéia slaps the air with a laugh. She knows
she is a Gift of God—her name marks her so—she knows also
that not all gifts are welcome. Her blackened kettle she will fill
with water from heaven harvested after dark—the old standpipe,
installed in secret by a compassionate communist, leaks blood:
light, swilched via the café, spits small fires to warm her hands.

And so each, expectant, braves the day. Jose prays a deluge
of tourists will discover this small square at the back of beyond;
Assuncão, fastidious, positions a plump calf in view of paving
and Columbano's fading eyes—a girl has to hedge her future;
only the hound is content to wait, to add his howl occasionally
to the constant conversation leaking each day from inner dark.

LEICESTER SQUARE

I am never quiet but always remain silent.
I know the many histories of the footfall
that cross my diverse paths but of such
I will never speak.
                              I am not, now, grand
but once I housed Hogarth, Reynolds,
Frederick, Prince of Wales: now I govern
the architecture
                              of those lives who call
me home—those whose small sigh-smile
breaks the moment they shumble across
to slink into my garden—old Llamas land.

I like to think they are reclaiming it:
such broken lives driven like leaves before
the sweeper's broom.

Tourists flock to me. Selfie sticks abound.
Others seek selves in a snort of white, unlit
passages offer solace to day-trip wives not
found in Fortnum's.
                              There they hope escape offers
hope, sanctuary from the mundane. Blind
to those who have fled before, who beseech
from blankets
                              blackened nails clawing after
a next fix, their pain ignored: semantically inclined
they jeer—*libertines, voluptuous gormandisers,*
yet some will lie, wordless: fragments in my garden.

I do not have a fountain thrusting heavenward.
My water rises after the last bar denies access.
   This is my flock. Their destiny. My square.

DEPARTURE

Warmed by the postcard of a red sun rising
over her village, its edges chafing a sodden
wool beret cowling her head where snatches
of childhood and reggae once slow-coasted
in a throng of black, orange, yellow, colours
that held her fast, taut body a waking-sleep
shifting on the slatted bench; one arm flung
across her face reveals a grin of white scar,
yet one more failure, the fifth since he died.

RETURN

Behind the skeletal pines they found her,
a huddle of rags, fingers plaited, the snow
-light lifting into the surprise of her smile,
how you greet an old friend you thought
had maybe emigrated, whose absence
knifed through you though his presence
at the time was simply accepted.
                              Moving her,
a coil of wind caught at the colours of her beret,
a thread snagged on the rough wood allowing
a creased card to drop onto the whitened earth:
    a red sun rising. A flame in winter.

Aftermath

This bog, this tidal mouth, this narrow gravel, allowed
a bridge, constructed, deconstructed, moved, allowed
ships to be moored in deep waters, allowed a flood
of foreigners, allowed free movement of merchants,
of goods, the displaced, dispossessed: allowed Boudica
to revel in the advantageous absence of a Roman
presence to raze the city, yet raised again, walled, defining
perimeters, changing, ever-changing.
                                        Londinium,
Lundenwic for the Angles, the Saxons Ethelberht,
Saebert, Saeberht, while Alfred aroused, rose, repulsed
Sweyn Forkbeard, established Lundenburh which gave
sway to Lundin, Lunden, Londen

burgeoning

burgeoning

burgeoning

burgeoning

burgeoning

LONDON

"Isn't it funny," Mr Farage said.

"When I came here 17 years ago and said I wanted to lead a campaign to get Britain to leave the European Union, you all laughed at me.

Well you're not laughing now."

BBC News 28 June 2016

The usual stench of piss not Vespasian taxed
in neon-lit Piccadilly this Circus of Westminster
where habitués recycle to these streets nightly
consumption of their chosen fermented amber

Fosters

while   TDK offers Audio Video Floppy…
and   Burberry Watches

pedestrian populations throng, always a throng, _____
even roaming-around-Romans thronged, all the XXXV,
but today they make their way beyond boundaries
where mere theatre is upstaged by professionals
appearing due west to hear a tidal mouth of narrow
attitudes spill lip service to a deserving electorate
hell-bent on destruction but hey-ho nearby the Abbey
offers prayers importuning Heaven for a safe election
referendum, transition, and we will be free as once
we were free of earphones and catholics but never
misogyny especially now as we need to by-pass smart
-phone addicts, joggers, shoppers, cyclists, tourists
crowding Victoria St. outside the *other place,* not
The Other but that relic of hierarchical heresy where
both dogs and dispossessed display abscessed legs
while inside the palsied limbs of a priest raise a white disc
whining at the elevation

Through Him
With Him
In Him

as surely as that son of Orpington Urban District was truly
elevated by S. Coast Colonel Blimps tilting UKIP banners
in that Year of Our Lord 2014,

Farage
Farage
Farage

promising economic emancipation once blacks,
browns and any frigging-johnny-foreigner-shade
-in-between were sent back so we could reclaim
those same jobs that we had all disdained to do

in the unity of British spirit
all glory and honour is his

until Brexit resignations incriminations FARRAGO.

Who gave orders to shrink the pink? Deny
my white child's heritage?

                    Oh, Farage, Farage.
Pistol and sword prised open the Protect
(huh!)—orates, diplomacy reduced dominions
to Common Wealth—tell that to Africa, India
or the N.E. denizens demanding devolution
—defeated, deflated—inflated as the bellies
of its citizens fed on white bread, seeking
the holy grail within the golden arches
courtesy of Mr. MacDonald while Jocks
strap themselves to Europe, Wales' slag (language!)
heaps are their own: N.B.. Aberfan, the NCB
more tight-fisted than the Krays, pro rata
given the size of each Firm, as for Ireland....
Which b.liar took credit for that piece
of peace agreement?
                    Why! Old Look At Me!

Ordure! Ordure!

1.

Oh, he could bowl a maiden over, Mo,
hit her for six, lost in the boundaries—
ever-changing according to gospels
spouted from the gargoyles of Westminster.

He knows how to devolve power, Friday's
never a good day—look at what happened
at Gaguita, the place of the skull—with Peter
he certainly had your head, bewigged or bald,

popularity's price—a-Maze-d as prisoners
rescinded their veto but T.B. was not to be
out-ranked—without doubt he is the most rank—
reduced you to tea lady but would have fully
concurred with your own last request: D.N.R.

2.

From this land of Buggery and Bingo
(though Kelly's Eye saw too clearly
lying in a field of buttercups 'n daisies)
came blind belief in WMD, rumour
(I know, Mo, it rhymes with tumour)
manufactured by the smooth tongue
of one B. toadying to good ol' US
two sons-of-a-gun, father 'n son,
and three B.'s make an unholy trinity
with which to chastise the Prophet's
followers—do not disguise intentions.
How right was Alistair to declare
We don't do God unlike dear old Basil,
he Hume dared to reprimand Tony's
contravention of canon law—but what's
a canon when we have bombs galore?

3.

In another city a child wakes
to a rat-a-tat-tat which is not a drum

4.

In council care a child lies awake safe
in the knowledge of the nightly rustle
on the stair—the hand slipped between.

5.

They will never learn, sodem: Sodom

oh white man in
gaberdine mac
who can carry
the cross in both
kensington high
or glasgow street
and not deny any
who speak hear
the cry of scots
who greet and both
old and young
who see their future

BLEAK?

DEMO

A stick
loosed
from its board

message
no longer
visible.

A blue line
thick
borrows

the domestic:
corners
images of tea.

No Polly
this kettling
it denies

splinter groups
limits
baton charges.

Corralling
animals incites
affirmation

in a gutter
the pack of three
featherlite, unused.

POW

One wore a fez of kilim fabric, assimilated and laughed
J*ust like that!*

One wore a jabellah from which he magic-ed streamers
to amuse children.

One wore the hijab in accordance with *Hadith* but bound
the newborn when the mother fell.

One wore a burkha to retain modesty but released it
to resuscitate her neighbour (male)

One wore a turban unwound it (RTA) to stem bright blood.
One wore a belt.

AND YOU ASK WHY?

I offer you bangla, reggae, ska, hip-hop.
You jeer. Shout those so friendly names
everyone can hear as I smile, answer to

paki, darkie, turban, nig-nog, wog, ape,
crow, sambo, coon, spade, Rastus, nip,
picaninny, ching-chong, chinky, slope,
jungle bunny, banana, kebab, slit eye,
        'cos I am the Oriel Kid. Geddit?

Your cricket you play on a smooth green,
we play in dirt roads, deliver like D'Oliveira.
C.B.E. not BBC.* Berlin '36, Jesse Owens
defeat Hitler. He run faster, jump longer,
we jump higher, work longer. We survivors
do whatever we have to: we prove it to you.

We even quote Shakespeare better than you.
In any Bombay brothel your whore will take
you in hand knowing a white man wears his
veneer of virtue, swears undying love, so she,
to the rhythm of your moans, wearily declares

Time shall unfold what plighted cunning hides:
Who cover faults, at last shame them derides.†

Her grandmothers adopted the same position
when the Raj swaggered in, whether Bombay,
Basutoland, Cameroon, Bechuanaland, B.E.A.
We all one under the skin that's what you say,
we say too. So now we take back our lands,
stay in your land, offer for your consideration

afro-saxon, windian, bean dipper, beach nigger,
wigger, won ton, bacon bit, shit palm, burd turd,
kango, blanco, whisky tango, jafaken, flat ass
perm sperm, MD, WT, Yang Guizi, 8 Mile, Egg,
    'cos you are the Crisco‡ Kid. Geddit?

* BBC—British Born Confused
† Cordelia in King Lear
‡ Crisco is a white vegetable oil product.

THE STATUS QUO

They are all gone now those oh-so-brave rebels
deserting the ship of state like the proverbial rat:
no Gove on hand to glove the chill from the edge;
no Farage—loudly trumpeting he knows the way
as his beer froths—only a blonde buffoon to shake
a head and loose a tongue which May cause her
regret in retaining both friends and enemies near,
adhering to the adage, one I keep close as my shirt
but closer still to my skin I keep the enemy within
surveillance.
    Forty years of communal alliance
diminished, absence of war relegated to history,
future negated in absence of plan. Ah, give me
Status Quo who began their heavy metal sound
circa the same time and to a man remained true
while we stomped to their music so loud refuge
was denied except in Angela's party who denied
the Right, the spirit flowed and she refused to obey
the law's letter preferring her own moral code
 Gib mir deine Flüchtlinge
Das Vaterland heisst alle willkommen.

(Does half-mirth and chuckle equal Merkel, Geoffrey?)
And where will we find another dear incisive you
now over that final hill? You who closely examined
our nation's condition with an eloquence that eluded
you're-not-laughing-now Farage (never one to be less
than gloating in victory.) We too have little laughter,
can only wonder who will now cry *Speech! Speech!*

Autopsy

...and what of that no longer spoken?